Ken

Ministry I _____ _____
(Aim Low)

Ministry Is a High Calling
(Aim Low)

Reflections of a Parish Novice

Kurt R. Schuermann

Geneva Press
Louisville, Kentucky

Book design by Sharon Adams
Cover design and illustration: Rohani Design

First edition
Published by Geneva Press
Louisville, Kentucky

This book is printed on acid-free paper that meets the American National Standards Institute Z39.48 standard. ♾

PRINTED IN THE UNITED STATES OF AMERICA

01 02 03 04 05 06 07 08 09 10 — 10 9 8 7 6 5 4 3 2 1

Library of Congress Cataloging-in-Publication Data

Schuermann, Kurt R., 1953–
   Ministry is a high calling : (aim low) / Kurt R. Schuermann.
     p. cm.
   ISBN 0-664-50149-4 (alk. paper)
   1. Pastoral theology. 2. Clergy—Office. I. Title.

BV4011.S3565 2001
253—dc21   00-55113

Contents

Acknowledgments

I would like to thank the members of the Zion, Bethel-at-Pond, Grace, Cuba, and First United Methodist Churches who made the journey toward authentic Christian community with me. I am particularly grateful for those kind people at Zion who endured my ministry back when I knew everything. I must give a special thanks to the staff of First United Methodist Church in Poplar Bluff, whose gifts make up for my many shortcomings.

I am greatly indebted to Edwin H. Friedman, whose book *Generation to Generation* (New York: Guilford Press, 1985) took Murray Bowen's ideas on family systems theory and applied them to congregational life. His seminars and writings were a source of inspiration and challenge. His death before the completion of his final manuscript was a loss to those who care about life in community.

I must thank my best friend in the ministry, Mark D. Williams, who made me laugh so hard during our frequent phone calls that I was able to experience the fresh air of grace for a moment. This book is filled with snippets of those phone conversations. Mark, you taught me <u>never</u> to <u>accept less than what was true and real.</u>

And finally, I am deeply thankful for my family, who have taught me most of what I know about life. My children, Erick, Drew, and Dana, have astounded me with the grace with which they have moved from town to town. Your individual gifts originated from a Source beyond your parents. Words are unable to express how blessed I am to have a life partner like my wife, Carol. <u>Her very touch has made me human.</u> After twenty years she still laughs at my jokes, while encouraging me to get some new material. Without her competent editing, this writing would be an incoherent mess. I love you, Bird.

Ministry Is a High Calling
(Aim Low)

Introduction

A Trip to the Dumpster

❄ ❄ ❄

I've just finished moving. This is not an unusual event in the life of a minister. I've moved five times in twenty years. My most recent move was unique, since it didn't involve moving to a new city, a new church, or a different set of responsibilities. This time, all I did was change offices. A remodeling program at my church necessitated the move. In actuality, I moved about fifty yards. To put a metaphysical spin on it, some of our biggest moves don't have to do with distance traveled. The biggest moves have to do with the geography of the soul. You can travel a long way while sitting still. I guess that's what happened to me.

The office from which I moved was in the older part of the church building. Built in the 1950s, my office was called the "Pastor's Study." It had a beautiful burnished metal plaque on the door which said it was the place where the pastor, well, studied. The room was even arranged for performing this task. A huge desk was surrounded by wooden shelves that went from floor to ceiling. I filled these shelves with books. I studied.

My new spot doesn't say "Pastor's Study" on the door. It merely says "Office." The sign is plastic. It is a modern office and has a spare and minimalist feel to it. There is an established place for a computer, but bookshelves had to be added as an afterthought. Overflow books sat in boxes for weeks. My book collection had to be pared down to fit my new surroundings.

How was I going to decide which books fit the shelves? Which ones to keep? Which to throw away? By size? By color? Past usefulness? Future promise? I had to handle each book and decide which ones had to go. It was a scholarly purge. As I went through them, I could document my past interests and certain "fads" my denomination passed through. I could also see how my book buying reflected my level of panic over the problems I found at each new church.

As far as I could tell, I was supposed to be at one time or another (or at the same time): a counselor, visionary leader, manager, fund-raiser, soul friend, church growth consultant, quality control expert, advertising executive, spiritual entrepreneur, prayer warrior, Bible scholar, covenant group leader, compelling preacher, resident theologian, CEO, and leader of an effective staff. No wonder I spend a lot of time feeling confused and inadequate.

Many books I handled during my library's purge had titles like *Ten Ways to Fund an Effective Church* and *One Hundred Ways to Increase Church Attendance.* Markings, margin notes, and highlighting seemed to suggest that I actually read these books. But strangely enough, my churches didn't always grow; the finances were usually adequate but certainly not spectacular. In fact, I can recall times when church attendance actually decreased after trying some things suggested in one book and finances became so strapped after implementing suggestions in another that raises weren't possible. What went wrong? What I really needed was a book entitled *Ten Steps to Finding Out What Ten-Step Books to Read.* I do know this: No worthy task in life can be contained in ten steps, or even a hundred. Life is not so easily out-lined. This is particularly true of the "God-life" we as ministers deal with. It seems that God might confound all our ten-step efforts by producing an eleventh step—just to let us know who's the Boss.

While I was lugging box after box of books to the dumpster, I came to a rather unflattering conclu-sion about myself—maybe I was addicted to "How to" books. Maybe I was addicted to the fact that I always wanted to be the guy with the answer quoted from the most recent book. What I needed was a twelve-step program to defeat my addiction to ten-step books. On the way to the dumpster, I was willing to take Step Number One—the real-ization that I was powerless over my addiction.

I had a friend in seminary who had a profound Quaker spirituality. He told me a story about a first-year seminary student who visited the study of a world-famous scholar. This scholar's study was filled with books. The shelves ran from the floor to the fifteen-foot ceiling. Ladders were attached to the bookcases to reach the books on the top shelves. The young student asked a typical question: "Wow, look at all these books! Have you read them all?" The scholar responded profoundly,

"Yes, but I stopped a while back because they weren't making me a better person." It seems there is a distinction made between knowledge held in books and wisdom.

I guess this is where this latest move has taken me—into some uncharted landscape of the soul. I'm hoping for a different viewpoint from this new vantage place. Like that scholar, I'm not sure all those ten-step books did very much for me in areas that really counted. As I once heard author and mentor Edwin Friedman ask, "What do you want, real life or propaganda?" Too often, I fear that I settled for propaganda by trying to make life fit into the outlines presented in books.

This is all to say that this book was conceived on the way to the dumpster. Therefore, I have no illusions about its permanence. I thought I might write about what I have found to be true since I threw away one hundred books. I have thought of this book as a lens that might help you to see clearly and therefore truly live. It is a slim volume, so it won't take up much room on your shelves. After reading it, you might want to share it or give it away. Ultimately, it is my hope that you will have no remorse if you have to toss it into the trash.

1

Ministry Is a High Calling (Aim Low)

✳ ✳ ✳

I know of a pastor who dressed in a suit and tie every day of his life. The only day he took time off was New Year's Day, and on this "break" he worked on his tax returns. Over the years I have known pastors who never dressed down because they didn't want their parishioners to see them "off duty." I have even heard about a pastor who wore a tie while cutting the parsonage grass. (I believe he removed his coat.)

There was a time in our Annual Conference when the prevailing fashion among clergy was to wear metal crosses around their necks. Every year the crosses seemed to get larger and more decorative. This fashion trend seemed to be another signal that we as clergy were always on duty. One pastor wore a cross that was so large and shiny that one of my friends named it "the Buick."

I realize that ministry is a big job and that it takes commitment. An argument *can* be made for wearing crosses as a witness. But I wonder if such dedication evidenced by always being "on duty" doesn't produce the opposite effect from what is intended.

Being a pastor is important; it should be in the top ten list of your priorities. It just shouldn't be number one. Your own spiritual life should be first (unfortunately, your job as a pastor doesn't always encourage your spiritual growth). Your family should be in there at number two, followed by a couple of passionate interests. Keeping your life in balance will help the people of your church identify with you and your common struggle of discipleship.

If wearing a metal cross around one's neck made an authentic pastor, then a simple catalog order would allow everybody to be the real thing. If you don't make being a pastor your highest priority, then you will probably come closer to being the pastor you need to be.

Don't Talk about Your "Call."
It Will Only Confuse People

You might be able to document the exact moment of your call to the ministry. No doubt this was a beautiful, dramatic, and life-changing event. You probably had to answer questions about your call and how it was validated to the people responsible for your ordination. This was the right moment to wax eloquent about your answer to God's call.

Once you arrive at your church, however, it is wise not to refer to this fact too often. This is particularly true when dealing with the group responsible for evaluating your ministry. Most people on that committee have *jobs,* and they probably won't be able to identify much with the divine origins of your calling. I grew up in a working-class neighborhood where people had jobs if they were lucky.

They respected what a job meant, because their hold on employment was tenuous. How are people like that supposed to evaluate you on the basis of your "call"? You need something more tangible than that. Your ministry is vital to the health of the church you have been called to serve. You have been placed in that congregation to help that group of believers develop and maintain an authentic Christian community. If you can do that, the people of the church will both recognize and validate your call.

In my experience, it is the least effective pastors who talk about their call. The logic seems to be: "Since I've been called by God, anything I do is right." Too many pastors view their service in a church as a time that allows them to do exactly as they please. But this is a great disservice to any group of believers. As a pastor, you are supposed to seek God's will for yourself and your church by gathering hints and clues scattered about among the people of God. Hanging on stubbornly to the claim that you were on the "right" path years ago probably indicates that you're off that path now.

You Will Be a Custodian

𝔉or a large part of your ministry, you will be a custodian.

Don't look for any higher, spiritual truth in this statement. I don't mean that you will be a custodian of sacred texts, or holy articles of worship, or souls. I mean you will be the person who cleans toilets, takes out the trash, and carries tables. While you shouldn't be the only one to do it—or even be expected to do it—you must not consider yourself above it. If everyone in the church is working, you should too. I have known pastors who wouldn't even carry their dishes back to the kitchen to be washed at the end of a potluck supper. Loading the dishwasher is an acceptable task even for someone with a degree from seminary. In this vein, cutting the parsonage grass is not demeaning to your status either.

At one of my churches the part-time custodian was seventy-five years old. When sudden snow-storms blew through our area on Saturday nights I couldn't bear to watch him shovel the snow, so I did it. At another church I built the fire in the wood stove. At still another church I followed the aging custodian, who had the beginning of Alzheimer's disease, into the restrooms, scrubbing the toilets for her while her mind wandered. This allowed her to stay on the payroll, giving her a much-needed supplement to her income until the ravages of the disease forced her retirement.

Human nature being what it is, I confess that I wasn't always happy scrubbing toilets and building fires on Saturday nights, but looking back I have a warm feeling about my custodial tasks. I was probably more a pastor scrubbing toilets with that aging custodian than any place else. My present church has a computerized thermostat that turns the furnace on without help. But I do miss building those Saturday night fires. It is, in my memory, a sweet time of recollection and spiritual refreshment. The warmth in the sanctuary on Sunday morning was the real thing—combining time, effort, and love.

If you just can't get to the place where you consider yourself a custodian, then call yourself a Levite. Being a Levite will put you in a long, ancient, and honorable line of people who labored to prepare sacred places for worship. Who knows—you might discover, as others have, that cleaning bathrooms somehow works around to cleansing your soul as well.

Don't Ever Use Any Words
You Learned in Seminary

These include, but are not limited to:

- liturgical renewal
- visioning
- the inner child
- paradigm shift
- postmodernism
- *sitz im leben*
- process thought
- empower
- the homiletical plot
- discernment
- tribal amphictyony
- any Greek word
- the name of a German theologian
- the name of *any* theologian

Those who do best in ministry stop talking like seminary students as soon as possible. Speaking "seminary-ese" works with a very tiny segment of the population. You left that group behind when you took your first church. In fact, if you continue to use it, the people will come to believe that you are remote, uncaring, and patronizing. Effective pastors are the ones who quickly learn to speak the heart-language of the people. This involves more listening than many pastors are willing to do.

All Ministers Are Interim

❀ ❀ ❀

If it hasn't happened already, it will happen someday. Someone in your church will say, "Preacher, I was here before you came, I'll be here after you're gone." Sometimes this claim is stated as a joke. Sometimes it is part of a bald-faced power play that hopes to derail your newest programming initiative. But take heart—while the first part of your parishoner's claim is obviously true, the second part is wishful thinking. You *might* outlast him.

Arriving at a church is a lot like jumping onto a moving train. Leaving a church is like jumping off the same train a few miles down the track. Both events can be both disorienting and painful. No matter how old your church, it has already been through more than you'll ever know. It will survive the sabotage of church members, new programming initiatives, and, yes, even your ministry. Christianity is nearly two thousand years old; your failures will not derail it. Your successes might even contribute a little to Christianity's spread. So, even as you plan for a long pastorate, realize that all ministers are interim. There's a certain peace to recognizing this fact.

6

Don't Take Things Personally, Even If They're Meant That Way

Mrs. Jones has just walked up to you after worship and is filled with concern. She says that she doesn't recognize her church anymore. She doesn't like the fact that you removed "prayer concern" time from worship. You removed it for several excellent reasons. It began to take up too much time and seriously interrupted the flow of the service. Besides, those shared concerns totally baffled and excluded visitors, who had no clue as to who was being spoken about. Mrs. Jones claims that you have totally ruined any sense of community that existed in the church. She turns on her heel and heads out to the parking lot.

Mrs. Jones caught you with your guard down in front of a large crowd. All you could manage by way of response was a muffled apology and meek smile. She probably slept great that night after getting this complaint off her chest. You don't sleep well at all; in fact, you replay her comments all night long. You think about them the next day as well. You berate yourself for letting Mrs. Jones's critique of your worship service knock you off stride. Even though you've had kind and supportive comments from many people, somehow Mrs. Jones has offset all the positives.

There are people who haven't liked anything that has happened in the church—ever. Why they continue to show up to be miserable is a deep and profound mystery. Therefore, a full understanding of Mrs. Jones and her need to criticize will never occur. The only light I can offer on the subject is that people like Mrs. Jones are actually *addicted* to the response they receive from you when they criticize the most vital and intimate parts of your ministry. Your hostile, nervous, defensive, or pleading response only feeds their addiction. If you play into their hands, their addiction, like all addictions, will require more potent and frequent hits for them to get "high."

It will take a lifetime in the ministry and incredible effort to get to the place where you don't lash out immediately to feed Mrs. Jones's addiction. If you can be calm in the face of her attack and not reactive, Mrs. Jones will be left needing to feed her addiction somewhere else. In a real sense, your calm response will make her go cold turkey. Therefore, it is perfectly acceptable to agree with Mrs. Jones—you *are* a complete moron. This will not be the response she is seeking and your calm response will put the monkey on her back, where it rightfully belongs. Although this may sound harsh, allowing Mrs. Jones to feel the pain of her addiction is the only way she can get well; it is the most caring thing you can do.

Whether You Admit It or Not, You Have Absolutely No Idea What Is Going On

Consider for a moment what goes on behind the scenes during an encounter with a typical parishioner. This parishioner you are meeting over coffee is being affected by a myriad of forces and factors. The person is being influenced by hormonal levels, endorphins, digestion, sleep patterns, challenges to the immune system, job stress, unresolved issues from families of origin, problems with children, a lingering headache, subcellular changes, financial difficulties, and the movement of the Spirit. How all these things interact is anybody's guess. Multiply the complexity of this one encounter by the interactions of all the people gathering for church and you must soon come to realize that you can't possibly have an idea of what's going on in your church.

When faced with such complexity, I try to remember what a friend told me about riding a motorcycle through dangerous, ever-shifting rush hour traffic. During confusing times on the motorcycle, he said, the rider must stay in the middle of the lane, drive predictably, signal far in advance of any turns, and be ready to take evasive action if necessary.

This advice could help you negotiate the crush of factors affecting your church members on Sunday mornings. When facing such an enormity of forces and factors beyond your control, the best course of action is to take care of what *is* under your control. Therefore, as you steer your way through the church members on Sunday mornings, drive predictably and don't make any sudden turns.

8

You're No Sigmund Freud:
Counsel by Rolodex

Some pastors fancy themselves to be counselors. Being an effective counselor is no small feat. I have even heard some pastors share their concerns about their "counseling load." You really shouldn't have a counseling load. Too often, I fear, pastors retreat to the role of counselor because the status of pastor has been demeaned by society. One pastor I know, when asked what he does for a living, answers "public relations." It is not wise to turn your commitment into merely being a spiritual member of the "helping professions."

Beyond that, your training and licensing and the realities of your schedule probably won't allow you to be a really effective counselor. Usually, in pastoral counseling, the one huge motivation for clients to get better is missing—the fee. If you feel inclined to be a counselor, you must get more training, another job, and better malpractice insurance. As a pastor, if you find yourself counseling people who are dealing with more than the normal issues of life's "rites of passage," you might want to reconsider.

Keeping business cards of talented and trusted counseling professionals in a Rolodex is not diminishing to your status. Transferring the trust you have to another person, one who is a better-trained counselor, will help you *and* the troubled church member.

Instead of being a half-baked counselor, why not decide to be a full-baked preacher of the gospel?

9

Show Up and Shut Up: A Ministry Strategy for the Parish Novice

You might want to copy and hang the following saying in several prominent places—on the bathroom mirror, above your desk, or on the refrigerator:

> *A strategy for ministry: Show up; shut up; listen carefully; speak the truth in love; hang around to see the outcome; don't be surprised when your outcome is something different from what you expected.*

In the above list, don't skip over or underestimate the power of showing up. Woody Allen once said that 80 percent of success in life is just showing up. To make ministry work, you must actually be present. Too often pastors spend their time in ministry "leaning." We either lean into the past trying to make our present church like our last one, or we lean into the future yearning for our next assignment.

Amazing things can happen when you actually decide to show up, bringing body, mind, soul, and spirit to meet your present circumstances. Once, during a particularly dark period of my life, the usual church challenges joined forces with a series of financial setbacks. A new transmission, new septic system, new furnace, and quarterly taxes had not only emptied my savings account but had struck hard at my children's college savings plans and the cash value of my life insurance policy. I vowed to stick it out.

At one point during this period I happened to be wandering through a section of the church building that was empty during the week. Turning the corner, I was startled by a church member who attended maybe twice a year. There was absolutely no reason for this man to be in this section of the church building on Tuesday afternoon. He held out a hundred dollar bill. He said that he had been thinking about making this contribution to the church for a long time. I took the money and managed to mumble a thanks. Then he said, "I wanted to give you something too." There in his hand was a second one hundred dollar bill.

Now admittedly the gift didn't fix my transmission, install a new septic system, repair my furnace, or pay my taxes. It did allow me to buy food until the next payday. Amazing things happen—events filled with beauty and grace occur when you decide to be present. For Christian followers, the incarnation is one of the central mysteries of faith in which God's word took flesh. In some way the incarnation didn't just take place once long ago. It can occur at some level to those who decide to "be" where they actually are.

10

Go to the Seminar, but Don't Believe
Everything You Hear

❄ ❄ ❄

Maybe this has happened to you: You're driving home from a seminar that has covered some aspect of church life—evangelism maybe, or contemporary worship. You're psyched up and filled with enthusiasm. The back seat is filled with all the books and videotapes you purchased at the seminar. On the seat next to you is a three-ring vinyl folder that holds the seminar's outline and your careful notes. And though the seminar, books, and tapes cost your continuing education allotment for the next three years, you're hopeful that *this* seminar will be the one to turn your church around.

Then it strikes you: The Church Seminar Letdown Syndrome. The first symptom usually hits about one hundred miles from home, as you realize that no one there is going to be as excited as you are. Next, you realize that what worked in the megachurch that held the seminar might not work at your home church. You realize that you might not have the gifts needed to implement the teachings from the seminar. You begin to berate yourself: "Why can't I have a megachurch that gives seminars?"

When this syndrome strikes you must remember that you were a *guest* at that church (and a paying one at that). The host church put on its best face for the guests. It is the church equivalent of putting out the best towels in the guest bathroom. If you were around enough, the perky, upbeat, enthusiastic seminar leaders would be tired, cranky, and uninspired from time to time.

What you may fail to realize is that the church giving the seminar is on the lookout for junior high Sunday school teachers, just as yours is. It seems that all churches throughout Christendom, whether high-tech megachurches, stately downtown churches, or white-steepled open country churches, are united in their search for teachers of young adolescents.

If only they had a seminar on how to find such teachers. . . .

11

How to Answer the Question: "How Big Is Your Church?"

❋ ❋ ❋

Pastors have to field this question on occasion. It is often posed by people who attend or minister to a really large congregation. They are usually secure in the knowledge that your answer will reflect a church smaller in membership and attendance than theirs.

Next time, just for fun, try this for an answer: "I really don't keep track, but I'm trying to whittle it down to a manageable size—ten tithing millionaires would be ideal."

This answer so goes against the grain of usual expectations that you will be able to move on without having to answer any more questions designed only to build up the ego of the one posing the question.

In the best-case scenario, your answer will be an invitation for everyone involved to investigate the need to ask such questions. Maybe we all could get to the place where congregations can be judged by more than seating capacity.

12

Goal Setting Gives God a Good Laugh

Setting goals is an appropriate mechanism for losing weight and producing your personal-best running times. However, I'm not certain goal setting lends itself very well to the production of authentic spiritual communities.

Goal setting used to be in vogue in churches—as if setting a goal had some miraculous power. This tendency seems to be on the wane, but I am still asked to fill in denominational reports concerning numerical attendance goals for the next year. Really now, am I supposed to know the future? Isn't the future pretty much hidden from view? If you must set goals, it is far better to set goals for your own behavior and activity than to try to predict the numerical outcome of the church year.

As Psalm 33 suggests, "If you want to give God a good laugh, trot out your plans and goals." In my ministry, I've found that every time I set a goal for an increase in attendance or membership the growth took place somewhere else—like the choir. Putting some goals down on paper doesn't change God's plans for your congregation at all.

13

Some Growth Is Cancer

Cancer is a disease that won't say no. During a cancer outbreak, malignant cells don't limit themselves. Cancer cells are totally self-centered, taking all available nutrients, refusing to cooperate with the other cells, and eventually pushing out the healthy cells. Cancer serves no larger purpose other than its own expansion. Eventually such unrestrained growth destroys the body.

Sometimes I get uneasy around too much talk about church growth. I often think that churches reflect American culture's obsession with size, glamour, and even celebrity. We probably need to liberate our churches from the clutches of the American dream.

Churches are growing, baptisms are up, and

talk of conversions is in the air. Seminars on church growth through worship, media, and even recreation have waiting lists. But sometimes I think—so what? A look at our culture shows that church expansion has made little impact. Does the growth of our churches mostly reflect the expansive and acquisitive nature of American culture? Churches seem to want bigger buildings, larger numbers attending, better landscaping, and off-street parking. If 500 in worship is good, then isn't 5,000 ten times better?

The Bible which we study was first produced and read by a tiny and persecuted band of outcasts. These outcasts were formed by the Word in the Bible to produce communities that offered an alternative to the organization and style of the surrounding culture. For these tiny communities to call themselves "the people of God" was a great cosmic irony. It is an altogether different situation when the wealthiest and most powerful people in history claim the title "the people of God." Too often this title finds easy confirmation in the growth of the congregation.

It would be interesting to find a church that said "no" to the addiction to more and bigger. Maybe we could get to a place where we could recognize and appreciate the small and subtle nudges to faithfulness God makes in all congregations. This would be true church growth.

14

Without a People, the Vision Perishes

¶I found this chart hidden away in the closet of a church I served:

WORSHIP ATTENDANCE CAMPAIGN

Worship Last Year	Attendance Goal	Attendance This Year
Week 1 336	400	292
Week 2 309	400	327
Week 3 318	400	301
Week 4 379	400	308
Week 5 328	400	381
Week 6 439 (Palm Sunday)	500	380
Week 7 635 (Easter Sunday)	800	672

During the attendance campaign, this chart was placed in a prominent place in the church. It amazes me that after the first two weeks of coming nowhere near the goal, someone continued to dutifully fill in the spaces. If I had been the pastor of that church during the time of the struggling crusade, I'm sure I would have suggested as calmly as possible, "Take down the darn chart!"

It seems that every church and every denomination wants visionary pastors these days. This emphasis on the "vision thing" has even spawned the strange word "visioning." Since visionary pastors are in demand, a glut of books has hit the market explaining how to become a "visionary."

The problem comes when the pastor develops a vision of his or her own and then delivers that vision to the church. I have known pastors who bring the same programming ideas to every church they serve, totally disregarding the change in context. I have known others who, within the first month of their arrival, meet with the church leadership and lay out exactly what needs to be done. I have known pastors who started to make plans to remodel the church offices as soon as they arrived. Pastor and people need to travel together as they seek a common vision for the church. We are a people of "the Way," which seems to suggest that the vision will be formulated slowly—step by step. If the vision is truly of God, pastor and people will receive it together. If you focus exclusively on *your* vision, you run the risk of traveling toward that vision all by yourself.

15

Youth Are Not the Future of Your Church—They're the Future of Somebody Else's Church

❀ ❀ ❀

There is nothing like ministry to youth for bringing anxiety into the life of your congregation. Society has managed to separate the age of possible childbearing from the time of financial independence by more than ten years. The result is the decade of adolescence, which is pretty much uncharted territory for both church and society. Not long ago, teenagers had vital roles both in society and in their family's survival. My grandfather, for instance, was apprenticed at age twelve and not long after that was bringing his paycheck home to help his fatherless household.

It would be hard to imagine a youth ministry of one hundred years ago surrounded by the anxiety that we have today. Reflecting on the present situation of the modern adolescent and his own daughter's obvious developing sexuality, one panicked father said to me, "Kurt, these kids are stupid and they've got, you know, *parts!*" Add to this reality lots of free time, a car, and a little spending money, and a lot of people will be looking to the leadership of the church to "do something!"

If your church adds a staff member, there will be lots of clamor to add a youth director. Someone will undoubtedly say something about youth being "the future of our church." This is, of course, not true, although no one will be able to contradict it. The fact is that most of your church's youth will eventually attend somebody *else's* church. A vital part of the ministry of the youth director you hire will be with the anxious parents of youth. These parents will need help in maintaining a flexible distance from their children. They need to stay in contact with these youth, but without becoming obsessive.

Just because you hire a youth director doesn't mean that the anxiety surrounding adolescence will disappear. Troubles will always arise and there will be much hand-wringing, during which many will wonder if the church is doing enough for youth. A part of your ministry will be with the youth director, who will have to defuse parental anxiety and live up to the church's request to "do enough." The average tenure of youth directors seems to be about three years. This is no doubt due to the fact that nobody could hold up very long with the ill-defined mandate to "do enough."

Most young people are probably under-challenged in their discipleship. You will need to encourage the youth director to challenge the youth to true discipleship without giving in to the rest of society's overheated and over-focused obsession. It will be difficult for adolescents to mature in their faith with a whole church trying to do everything for them.

16

How to Tell the Difference between a Member and a Customer

✳ ✳ ✳

Living as a part of the Christian community involves a change of heart and perspective, which moves a person from being self-centered to a place where the needs of the entire community can be considered. This change is enormous and moves forward in a series of jerky starts and stops. This transition is, simply put, not a smooth one.

People in your church will bring you suggestions about what they think needs to be done. These suggestions can range from ideas about outreach to concerns about the wallpaper in the women's restroom. Sometimes these requests represent real insights from a heart touched by Christ. Often, however, these suggestions reveal only a hard heart that seems to say, "I want this done *my* way." There is a time to challenge suggestions that don't reflect the best interests of the group; in so doing, you can help the person bringing the suggestion to grow.

You must also realize that you cannot fight every battle. Although it may not be a priority at the time, still it is acceptable to change the wallpaper in the women's restroom just because someone wants it done. Even the best members should be considered customers from time to time. As customers, they pay the bills and fill the pews, and are always right. Your challenge will be to choose your battles. In so doing, you must be able to figure out if the person you are talking to is at that moment a member or a customer.

17

There Are No Steps to Church Growth

Growth is a mysterious process and aims to stay that way. No one understands all the factors that contribute to growth. If we consider the growth of the human body, growth includes: genetics, nutrition, environment, exposure and resistance to disease, nurture, care, hormones, freedom from accident, the workings of all the organ systems, vitamins, minerals, and the delicately balanced interactions of all of these.

Church growth is at least as mysterious as the growth of a single human being. No one could possibly write a book that could account for every factor that would result in a church that grew numerically. Certainly no book could produce the intricate order and arrangement needed. Church growth "how to" books include those tangible factors observed by the writers. But there are many subtle contributing factors the authors never dreamed about.

When you were growing up, you didn't have to plan too much for it. You controlled only the factors you could, like rest and nutrition. A big part of the growth process was taken care of without your awareness, thank goodness. Even if you had really worked and planned to grow a body, no doubt you'd have blown the whole process.

Sometimes your churches will grow. Sometimes they won't. Sometimes churches will grow in spite of you (and maybe you'll write a book about it). However, sometimes no matter what you do, nothing will cause your church to move up one tick in membership or attendance. Even so, it is still possible to have a fulfilling and authentic ministry.

Most readers of this book have already stopped growing physically. You need to appreciate the wonder of your body as it matures, maintains, and sustains itself. Don't lose your sense of wonder about your church, even if it seems to be on a plateau.

18

Confrontation Is an Art

Shortly after I was first assigned to my present church, I wandered around trying to grasp the layout of the building. During this journey, I heard strange noises coming from behind some closed doors. I peered into the room and saw several people training for some form of the martial arts. I wondered why this church allowed such an activity in the building. Inquiring further, I discovered that the class was taught by a church member. Even knowing this fact could not stop me from quietly trying to figure out how to oust the martial arts from the church, leaving an empty room to be used for more "appropriate" activities.

I returned to the room, hoping to find a moment to speak with the instructor. I felt that I should be the one to tell him that the days of the church being used for "fight training" were numbered. Sitting on a chair at the back of the room, I discovered that the students were studying Aikido. The sparring I saw was different from the kind I was used to seeing on television. For instance, there were no chops, hits, or kicks. In fact, all the movements were flowing, resembling ballet or gymnastics more than any type of fighting.

As the instructor demonstrated one of the moves, which involved a graceful pivot, he informed the class that in Aikido the concept of being an "opponent" did not exist. What other martial arts called an "opponent," Aikido called a "partner." Indeed, the instructor's graceful pivot had blended with his partner's attacking energy and allowed him to nullify it. Both instructor and partner had ended up standing side by side, both looking in the same direction, with the instructor's hand on his partner's wrist. "From this position," the instructor explained, "you can see the world from your partner's point of view."

This was a great learning moment for me. When leading a church the pastor must take strong stands, and for most of my ministry this meant confrontation face-to-face. The Aikido instructor suggested an alternative. Sometimes it is wise to blend with an antagonist, even standing side by side to try to see things from his or her perspective. Aikido taught me that there are a variety of ways to take a stand; confrontation is an art that can be learned.

Needless to say, the Aikido class stayed in place.

19

Embrace This Mystery: Sometimes People Don't Do What's Good for Them

The first two chapters of Genesis tell how God placed the first human beings in the midst of paradise. By chapter 3 the primal couple had lost everything because they thought they knew more about living than God did. They lost everything because they listened to a snake. Somehow, *their* problem has become *our* problem.

One of the greatest examples of the brokenness of human beings is that people don't always work for their own benefit. This problem doesn't stop at the church door. People will often work in ways that are not in their best interest. In all likelihood, they will not work in your best interest or the best interest of the church, either. These people are sane and intelligent, but something is stirring beneath the surface. Reason doesn't work in these situations.

Pastors don't always know what is best, either. One thing is for sure—as early as Genesis 3, paradise is no longer an option. Although human beings were made for paradise, all of us must live out our lives somewhere else. The gap between the deep longing for paradise and the limitations of reality is the peculiar habitation of the pastor.

The church you are serving is not paradise. The one you are longing to serve won't be paradise either. If you are absolutely sure about moving to a new church, you need to slow down. In the spiritual history of the human race, getting exactly what one asks for has often turned out to be a curse.

20

A Prophet May Be a Pain in the Neck, but Not Every Pain in the Neck Is a Prophet

❧ ❧ ❧

There is a time to preach against society's evils; you must remember, however, that the prophets of old seldom had a group of long-term listeners as you do. Amos may have gotten away with calling some people "cows of Bashan," but you cannot. If you preach prophetically, you must let it be known that you are preaching to yourself as well. You are a part of that local congregation, and as such, you are implicated in the same societal problems as your listeners.

When I was a boy growing up in St. Louis County, Missouri, congregations were struggling with their witness in the face of the realities of the Vietnam War. Did the church believe that the war would halt the spread of communism? If we spoke out against the war, could we be in ministry to the parents whose children were fighting the war? If we didn't agree, could we at least remain together as a Christian community?

I recall a young associate pastor, fresh out of seminary and endowed with a passion for prophetic preaching, railing against the "military-industrial complex" that rained death on the children of Vietnam. The problem was that many of the people who were in church that day worked at McDonnell Douglas, a major defense contractor. What did the preacher want those people to do—quit their jobs? What the preacher *didn't* do was admit that he was a part of the problem. He could have offered to return the part of his salary that came from the tithes of McDonnell Douglas church members, but he did not.

This memory from my boyhood demonstrates that it is not wise to set yourself up against the people of your church. Just because a preacher is a pain in the neck, complaining constantly, doesn't make him or her prophetically correct.

21

Your People May Build You a Pedestal, but Don't Ever Climb Up on It

✳ ✳ ✳

The trip up may be enjoyable, but the trip down is sure to be painful—and a whole lot faster. Although it may be initially appealing, you really don't want the people to idolize you.

This is important to remember when you are collecting compliments about your excellent sermons or accolades about how you saved the congregation from total ruin. Inevitably, some of those who thought you were the church's savior will develop a quite different opinion of your ministry. You can save yourself some pain if you don't believe all the compliments in the first place. In any religious world view, there is only room for one savior, and you aren't him. Creating idols and worshiping them has always placed people in a precarious spiritual place. This is particularly true if the idol is the pastor.

Don't Take the Ministry Too Seriously

I was once in a meeting with a group of ministers and the resident bishop. Although I can't quite recall the reason for the meeting, I can vividly remember the oppressive heaviness of the gathering. Whatever the stated reason for the meeting, the gathering soon degenerated into a spiritual competition in which we each tried to convince the Bishop of our insight and ability. Brother Fred's church was growing so fast that temporary buildings had to be set up to handle the overflow. Sister Sarah's church was not only growing faster than Fred's, but her church was growing without watering down the gospel. Everyone tried to display their talents to impress the Bishop and maybe even get a promotion. I was in the groove with everyone else, trying to show the Bishop who the *really* effective pastor was. One pastor spoke what was on everyone's heart. He said, "I take my ministry very seriously" and proceeded to tick off a lengthy list of journals he read regularly.

We were a serious group; that could not be disputed. But driving home I wondered where our seriousness was leading us. All the glowing reports about the progress in churches we served couldn't possibly be accurate. If they were, our denomination would have shown extraordinary growth instead of decline. I wondered what would have happened if someone had said to the Bishop and those ministers gathered, "I take my ministry playfully." In some ways playfulness, like that of a child, comes closer to the attitude Jesus envisioned for his followers. Play, when you think about it, is good for children (and the followers of Jesus). It adds joy and contributes to growth.

Ministers know that there is a permanent gap between what is and what should be. All the seriousness in the world won't close that gap even an inch. Humor and playfulness in the face of this truth is an honest effort to live with reality. The biblical word for this type of perspective is "grace."

23

You Can Be Creative, but You Don't Have to Be an Original

I was in the United Methodist ministry for twenty years before it dawned on me that the number of Wesley's fifty-three *Standard Sermons* was more than just an interesting doctrinal coincidence. Publishing fifty-three sermons enabled his preachers to have a sermon for every Sunday of the year.

In other words, while it was certainly acceptable to modify existing sermons, the idea that one must preach an *original* sermon every Sunday is a relatively recent idea. Along with wanting a pastor who is dynamic, visionary, and young, most churches want a creative pastor. We all hope that our sermons are creative and dynamic, but it may be wrong-headed to blindly follow the rest of society's obsession for what is new. In some ways, we are called to re-present what was handed down to us. We're simply not supposed to be making this stuff up.

Sometimes we forget that preaching is part of an oral tradition—akin to storytelling. In oral traditions good stories are borrowed, modified, and even elaborated on. You should borrow from other preachers, giving them credit if you can. As one fellow traveler in the ministry once said, "When better sermons are written, I will preach them." This seems to be a sane and sensible approach to the weekly preaching task.

24

Ministers Are Slow-Moving Targets

Imagine the pastor processing down the center aisle of the church for the start of worship. Notice the slow and majestic cadence. Now imagine the preacher with a target on his or her back—a slow moving target. There are people who won't rest until they get their "shot" at the pastor. These "shots" can range from the trivial to the tragic. The pastor is bombarded with demands.

I once heard a story Ed Friedman told on this very subject. He was speaking to a mixed group of physicians and pastors concerning certain universal processes that can facilitate or inhibit the healing process. In order to help physicians understand the pastor's life, he painted this vivid picture: "Imagine seeing all your patients at once."

That's exactly it for pastors—no waiting room, no receptionist, no private room for a little one-on-one time. A person's concern about a terminally ill spouse can come on the heels of a complaint about the temperature in the choir loft.

There is probably no way to change this, as long as two or more are gathered on Sunday morning. But Friedman's vivid image, once appropriated, should at least lead to an understanding of what is actually taking place.

25

Beware of Angstide

❀ ❀ ❀

When I first started in the ministry there was a season of the church year called Kingdomtide, which stretched from the end of Pentecost season to the beginning of Advent. Somewhere along the way this season disappeared, so Pentecost is now one long stretch of time that cries out for interruption.

One of my friends proposes a new season for the church year—Angstide. This season roughly corresponds to September, October, and the first two weeks of November. To reflect the meaning of this season, the most appropriate liturgical color would be gray.

This season is a real period of angst-producing events for those in the ministry. This is a time of real, hard, make-or-break-your-ministry work. It is the season of the annual finance campaign, committee nominations, and finalizing plans for Thanksgiving, Advent, and Christmas. There are no religious holidays during this time to give an infusion of spirit and good feelings into your congregation. Many things are pressing during this time, but there is very little help to be found. Most of the church's key leaders are still in the summer vacation mind-set and are simply not around. Angstide and its challenges may reveal more about the state of your soul than the more traditional season of Lent.

You must prepare for Angstide in August and you must train for it like a warrior going into battle. Perhaps you could make an "Angstide Wreath," one that invites you to extinguish a candle every week instead of lighting one. Angstide will try your soul, but you can get through it if you start preparing your heart for it during the heat of August. Be of good cheer; you will notice the Angstide pressures finally easing about the time you're carving the Thanksgiving turkey.

26

She May Be Orange, but Her Problem Is More than Skin Deep

✳ ✳ ✳

Imagine a patient in a hospital. Her skin is bright orange. Doctors examine her carefully. They look at her skin, even take samples of it to look at it under a microscope. They can find no reason why her skin is orange.

It doesn't take a diagnostic genius to figure this out. Although her skin is orange, the source of the problem is in an organ system far away. She has a bad liver or gall bladder. No one could have determined this by studying her skin in isolation.

This same principle applies to church life. For example, a situation arises in the choir. Two of the choir members claim that the music is too fast or too slow, too contemporary or too traditional. You react quickly, asking the music director to make some changes to accommodate the tastes of these two. Three weeks later you discover that the choir members in question have been having major problems with their children; their problems at home have spilled over into the choir. In this case, you have merely treated the symptom, never reaching the primary site of the disease.

Now you have created a real problem. The choir director is sorely distressed that you intervened in his or her area of ministry when nothing was wrong. For the next quarter, you will hear nothing but heavy, Germanic organ music. It will be your penance for not looking beyond appearances to the source of the problem.

27

Most Theological Books Were Written While Looking in the Rearview Mirror

Have you ever noticed that most of your real blessings and the real leaps in growth as a disciple were recognized only after you passed them? It is only by looking back that you realize what actually happened. I suppose that's why we use the word "reflection" to describe our ponderings and realizations.

Most books we read as ministers are just that—reflections. Whether in the most technical systematic theologies or the more basic "how to" books, the author is looking back on what has worked or what has been experienced.

The trouble is that we don't live life like that—backward. We live life looking and moving forward. A lot of books tell us what happened or what worked in the past, but they don't necessarily help with the path ahead. That is why there is often some unexplained "slippage" between what we read and what actually happens in our ministry. You can learn from the past; it just can't be reproduced.

28

Play Stupid

⁋In the life of the church, it is usually better to ask more questions than to give quick answers. As leaders of congregations, we are often too quick to give an answer before all the information is in. Inevitably new information arises that has a bearing on the situation, causing reversals and backpedaling. Giving an answer before the true nature of the question is understood doesn't make you look smart, but rather just the opposite.

Give yourself a break from being the person with all the answers. Take a week and vow to ask questions more often than you give answers. Don't give an immediate response to a question even if you know the answer. You might want to take the old *Columbo* detective show as your model. As you may recall, Lieutenant Columbo never worried about looking smart. He just asked questions until the truth was finally revealed. By the end of the show, the hapless-looking Columbo had figured out everything.

Try wandering around your church building with the intention of only asking questions. A week of questions will provide you with a wealth of new information to inform your decision making.

Playing stupid is hard, but it can be liberating. If you follow Columbo's model, you may end up looking smarter than ever.

29

Beware of the Ones
Who Meet You at the Train

This bit of wisdom was given to me by an older retired preacher. The reference to the train shows that this observation must have traveled across the years; yet its teaching is still valid.

Basically this gem of wisdom refers to those who meet you first—even while the moving van is being unloaded. Most early arrivers have good hearts, willing hands, and a pie. There are others, though. These people come just a few steps behind, don't carry a box, and certainly don't bring a pie. All these people bring is information. They warn about factions, but assure you of their total support. When you first arrive at a church, it is hard to tell who is working for the ministry of the church and who is against it. The chronically displeased seldom bring a pie.

My family and I arrived at a church that had a reputation for conflict. A woman from the church met us "at the train." She assured me she understood the church's difficulties and had insight into the factions. She promised me that she was behind me "one hundred percent." There was no pie in sight.

Some months later, when the squabbles for which the church was known materialized, the woman kept her promise. She was behind me all right—so far behind me that her support could not be detected.

30

You Cannot Make People Get Along

❦ ❦ ❦

Part of the pastor's job is putting out the brush-
fires of discontent that break out in the congregation from time to time. Although it is difficult to
find this important task written down in any offi-
cial list of pastoral duties, the job is vital. Sometimes your arrival at a church will be the event
that causes problems to present themselves. Even
when things appear to be going well, long smol-
dering resentments can suddenly reignite. In fact,
when things are going particularly well, you
should be particularly watchful. Animosity can
suddenly flare up after having gathered fuel for
years. Any little spark can get a real conflagration
going.

You will recognize the fact that you have been

placed in a difficult position when you feel the anxiety as intimately as the angry parties. In fact, you might feel it more intensely than those involved. Friction within the congregation can grow into a consuming fire that can cost you your job!

You must know that you cannot make people get along. You simply do not have that power. As best you can, you must try to get the unhappy people to talk to each other with your moderating presence nearby. You must not get between them. You have the same challenge as all firefighters—extinguishing the flames without getting burned.

31

Remember, Ministry Is Just a Gig

❊ ❊ ❊

If baseball players, salesmen, and recording artists can go into a slump, so can you. There will be weeks when everything you say seems to be the wrong thing. There will be months when your preaching is as dry as a church finance committee meeting. There will be times when every programming initiative turns to mud. There will be seasons of life when your prayers fall to the ground with a thud. To be honest, I was in the throes of a ministerial slump for about five years. This is not an exaggeration or a joke. This is hard truth.

In sports and in ministry, the typical reaction to a slump is to try harder. A little extra practice can help in a minor downturn. This may involve more time in sermon preparation, or a couple of visits to the spiritual powerhouses in your life, or a seminar. But trying harder will not help the crushing career-threatening slumps. Trying harder only seems to push you farther down the road in the wrong direction.

A deep slump requires radical action. This can involve doing less or completing the usual tasks in radically different ways. When I was in my deepest slump, I repeated the following mantra: "Hey, it's just a gig." Eventually the mantra did the trick. I slowly moved out of the slump, probably because the mantra took the focus off of me and my performance. I stopped thinking about my ministry and how I was doing all the time. As Yogi Berra said about slumping hitters, "You can't think and hit at the same time." Eventually the natural grace and timing necessary to ministry will return.

32

New Blood Seldom Cures a Sick Body

There is an excellent chance that at least once in your ministry you will be asked to help heal a sick church. The ailments manifested by sick churches can range from mild-but-chronic to near-fatal. A lack of musical talent resulting in uninspired anthems can be a chronic aggravation but certainly not a life-threatening problem. However, a long history of poor worship attendance may just be one of a church's symptoms that reflect a slowing spiritual heartbeat. Not surprisingly, those churches on life support are looking for heroic measures and miracle cures. Sometimes the pastoral search committee will express the need for new blood.

Remember, however, that new blood seldom

cures a sick body. A body with a diseased heart will *still* have a diseased heart, no matter how much new blood is transfused into it. I served a church where the people saw little value in Christian education. In fact, it was this church's habit to eliminate Sunday school altogether during the summer months! After years of effort on my part, trying to repair attitudes and rebuild programs, the weak pulse that I took as a sign of life quickly faded when I turned my attention to other matters. Somewhere along the line, you will probably learn about the limited healing power of new blood—especially if you ever find yourself in the position of *being* that new blood.

The Path You Have Taken Is the Right One, So Why Haven't You Walked It?

We all know somebody from high school or college who didn't appear to be as smart or as charming as we were, but who went on to make a bundle of money and retire by age forty. It is a certainty that this person will show up at various gatherings and reunions. Wouldn't you? He will park his new Jaguar in a prominent spot and move through the party in a suit that costs more than *all* the clothes you own. He also tends to drop in on you—"just to see how you're doing." His clothes and new car will grate on your spirit because you've just stayed up all night trying to figure out how to stretch your budget to buy your son a new pair of thirty-two-dollar football cleats.

You remind yourself that you have eschewed

financial reward for spiritual gain. But your reminder falls on your own deaf ears. As you consider how your old friend can actually live the lifestyle of the rich and famous, some ugly thoughts may come to mind involving your friend, the Jaguar, and an eighteen-wheeler. With the arrival of these thoughts, your spiritual riches are reaching the level of bankruptcy, along with your finances.

The truth of the matter is that you have chosen the right path, but you haven't really walked it. The spiritual walk involves the willingness to enter into the fire of personal transformation. Too often, we pastors settle for being a middle manager who merely runs the denomination's local franchise. The goal of a spiritual life is being able to see the world as it truly is, without gloss or phoniness. If you can see clearly, if only for short periods, then your walk is worth it. A person who can see is rare, and such beings are rich in the best sense of the word. History shows that no one who truly walked this spiritual path ever wished to turn back.

34

The *Real* Church Year

Everyone who is in the ministry has an outline of
the church year imprinted on his or her brain.
Moving from Advent through Pentecost, the
church year reflects a certain eternal predictabil-
ity as the church celebrates the mighty acts of
God. Even if you serve a nonliturgical church,
some holy days like Easter and Christmas are still
observed. You can usually tell when the church
holidays arrive: people who work at churches are
stressed, while ordinary members are experienc-
ing inspiration and peace.

How you see the church year is not how the
church membership sees it. Listed below is the
church year as viewed by a typical church member. There will be some variations due to climate

and geography, but the basic precepts are accurate.

January	*Entire month off: Too cold to get out.*
February	*Entire month off: Colder*
March 7, 14, 21	*Off: Out of habit.*
March 28	*Palm Sunday: Attend: Child waving palm branches and singing. Bring camera and jostle for front seat.*
April 4	*Easter: Attend.*
April 11	*Off: Tradition to skip the Sunday after Easter. Let the ones inspired by Easter fill the pews.*
April 18 & 25	*Off: Already went in April. Don't want to be considered a zealot.*
May 2	*Off: Communion Sunday takes too long, have to get up and walk to front, leaving comfortable seat.*
May 9, 16, 23, 30	*Mostly Off: Pick one to attend so visitation committee won't drop by. Check son's traveling basketball schedule.*
June, July, August	*Off: Summer vacation. Get close to God on back of bass boat or witness for Christ with good sportsmanship on golf course.*

September 5	*Labor Day weekend—Off: Last weekend with family (must keep priorities straight).*
September 12	*Off: Not back in the habit yet.*
September 19 & 26	*Off: Annual pledge drive—tired of being preached at about money.*
October 3	*World Communion Sunday—Off (see May 2). Football tickets to pro game. Must get there early for tailgate party. Builds team spirit. Important!*
October 10 & 17	*Off: Daughter's soccer league games.*
October 24	*Off: Bowling tournament. Team is counting on me! (Reminder: league fees are due).*
October 31	*Off: Must get away. Stress. Pace is killing me.*
November 7 & 14	*Off: Deer season.*
November 21	*Thanksgiving Sunday—Attend: Good to be thankful. Improved snacks during fellowship hour.*
November 28	*Off: Over the river and through the woods to Grandma's house we go.*
December 5	*Communion Sunday (again!)—Off: Don't get how Communion fits in with Jesus' birth (see also May 2).*
December 12	*Attend: Children singing in church. Cute.*

December 19	*Sunday before Christmas—Attend: Don't wish to appear ill informed about remodeling project in Fellowship Hall.*
December 26	*Sunday after Christmas—Off: Are you kidding? Went on Christmas Eve. All that Christmas stuff has worn me out!*

35

The Spirit Is Self-Organizing

ℬ ℬ ℬ

ℐ have a friend in the ministry who has a sign on the wall of his office that reads: *Anyone who thinks this church isn't in chaos doesn't understand what's going on.*

Don't be too surprised if from time to time your church seems to be on the edge of chaos. While your first response may be to panic, keep in mind that chaos is often preliminary to and the indication of some new, higher organization occurring in your church.

When I first began in the ministry, the church was organized into various boards, committees, and work areas. Through this process we tried to force God's activities into our preconceived patterns. Chaos can occur when this structure of committees is challenged and ultimately reorganized by God. Trust this: The Spirit is self-organizing and will provide everything necessary to accomplish its task. A new, true, and startling spiritual organization is coming to pass in your church if you and the people of the church will allow it. If you are in tune, the Spirit will give you the vantage point to view the beautiful new symmetry of your congregation.

36

Be Alert When Someone Says,
"Well, It's the Bride's Day!"

❀ ❀ ❀

I only perform weddings for church members and, believe me, that's enough. Early in my ministry—in the name of evangelism—I would perform a wedding for anyone who would sit through my pre-marriage counseling sessions. This policy ended when I served a picturesque white clapboard, steepled church in the countryside near a large suburb. It seemed like every bride and her mother thought that this sanctuary would provide an ideal backdrop for the wedding spectacle they were planning. The number of weddings began to anger the organist and I realized that unless I quickly learned to play the organ, my wedding policy had to change. Really, the church of Christ had to be more than a prop and a homey background for wedding photos.

Few things that a pastor encounters have as much potential for demonic activity as the modern wedding. The sacred act of covenant can be lost in a maze of logistics and planning. You will need to recognize that some parents of the bride have been envisioning this event since their daughter's first steps. If you come to a point of contention during the wedding planning, you must realize that the parents of the bride will try to use the "Well, it's the bride's day" argument. This statement is viewed as the atomic bomb of arguments, destroying all opposition.

Once I was showing a bride-to-be and her maid of honor the sanctuary for an upcoming wedding. They went off by themselves and were feverishly discussing the merits of the sanctuary, trying to decide if this place was a worthy site for the wedding. The maid of honor delivered the outcome of their discussion: "Could you move that thing?" That "thing" was the cross! I nearly swooned and I believe that I heard the demons wail. Don't berate yourself if occasionally you dread a wedding.

I don't know how it occurred that the bride's

opinion took over God's place in wedding ceremonies, but it has. And photographers and wedding consultants have taken the pastor's place as
director. You must keep a sane perspective on this
or weddings will drive you mad. Once, during the
planning of a particularly elaborate wedding, the
father of the bride asked what my typical fee was.
I answered, "Oh, I don't know. It varies, usually
about ten percent of what the caterer is paid."
It was intended as a joke, but the look on that
father's face showed that he didn't consider it a
laughing matter. Perhaps the wedding costs had
already stretched his ability to pay to the limit.
Paying the preacher was just one more expense to
be taken care of.

I felt a little sad about the whole situation. I
certainly didn't need the money if it was going to
be just one more expense to be endured. I did
experience a twinge of remorse about a society
that seemed to think that what was essential to a
wedding could be bought and paid for. The depth of
commitment that is the basis for a successful married life cannot be covered by a check or put on
MasterCard. I'm not sure how one conveys that
truth.

37

Most Ministers Think They Are Great Preachers. Experience Shows This Isn't So

ℐt is rare to find a preacher who doesn't think that he or she is God's gift to sermonizing. It is even difficult to discover a preacher who admits to needing improvement in this area. But experience shows that even adequate preachers are fairly rare.

What is it that keeps us as preachers from having a healthy evaluation of our preaching? Once, during Lent, as a sign of solidarity, all the churches in our district were going to study and preach on the same scripture verses. Sermon starters were to be prepared by one selected pastor in the district and then circulated. Who was going to do it? Those gathered were shocked when the absolutely worst preacher in the district volunteered. His reasoning was, "I need to do this, because I'm good."

In fairness, this pastor was not without gifts as a visitor and organizer, but he simply could not preach. How could this otherwise competent pastor be so blind to his weakness in this one area? Furthermore, the grapevine revealed that each of the other pastors in the district (including me) thought that he or she was the one for the job.

To really grow as a preacher, you must at least entertain the thought that you are not yet a good preacher. The Buddhist tradition seeks, as an outcome of enlightenment, what is called "the beginner's mind." According to this teaching, in the beginner's mind all things are possible and yet to unfold. By contrast, the expert's mind is crowded and encumbered, pushing out both perspective and possibility. Humbly seeking to have a beginner's mind wouldn't be a bad way to start the weekly task of sermon preparation.

38

Don't Be a Gossip

At all costs, you must keep confidences and avoid gossip. Although it is difficult to keep these issues clear in your mind in the midst of the challenges of day-to-day church life, you must try. The following rule of thumb is one I use to help keep these issues straight:

> *A confidence is something someone tells you about himself or herself. Gossip is something someone tells you about somebody else.*

This rule is only a starting point, but it is a good and necessary starting point. I do know for a fact that in this strange and interconnected world, a violated confidence or an undealt with bit of gossip will come back to haunt you and your ministry. The mishandling of confidences and gossip will always strike your church at its most vulnerable spot, where the greatest amount of damage can be done.

39

Don't Hang Out with Too Many Ministers.
This Will Undoubtedly Mess You Up

To see things clearly, what we need is perspective. If you hang out only with ministers, you will probably not get the distance and perspective you need to see clearly the challenges you face. While I have good friends in the ministry and have appreciated the support of ministers, these friends are more likely to empathize with my problem than to challenge me. Those who even begin the task of ministry tend to have a certain outlook. Seminary training and years in the parish tend only to confirm that outlook.

I have found that I am more likely to be challenged by people in fields that appear to have little to do with the ministry. One friend astounded me with tales of his start in the insurance business. He began with no clients, hitting the streets with nothing but his ambition and a little book that contained his company's premiums for car insurance. Now, twenty years later, he has thousands of clients. He reminded me that there is an entrepreneurial aspect to ministry. Another acquaintance was a literature teacher. He gave me poems to read and kept me abreast of new books that were published. He challenged me to refine my ability to tell stories. Yet another friend ran a major business enterprise. Over the years, his business was challenged to change with the times. He helped me not to whine about the fact that things "weren't the way they used to be." This tendency to whine is common to church life. My business friend could not allow himself the luxury of whining. From him I learned to be challenged by change rather than intimidated by it.

The distance we need to gain perspective comes from insights that are hard to receive directly. Much of what we need to know comes as we overhear others discussing the real challenges of their lives. One key to an authentic ministry is to associate with a wide circle of acquaintances in order to "eavesdrop" on what they are saying and glean bits of truth that will enhance our effectiveness.

40

Learn to Write "Talking"

❅ ❅ ❅

Many years ago, when I was still able to stay awake past 10:00 P.M., I was a fan of *The Tomorrow Show*. This show began after Johnny Carson's *Tonight Show* signed off. Tom Snyder was the host of this show, and one night he was reviewing his career as a television journalist. He said that his greatest talent was that he could write the way people talked.

Somehow, even though I had no idea then that I was headed for the ministry, this statement struck me as a profound truth. I tucked it away in some dark corner of my mind, saving it for just this moment. What Tom Snyder said was that there was a fundamental difference between print journalism, which was read, and television journalism, which was listened to. This is a vital distinction and one that preachers must take to heart.

Most of us who are in the ministry probably attended seminary or Bible college. Although there were classes in preaching, in which we spoke, most of our grades were based on our writing. We wrote papers and produced essays for tests. This trained us to think in a linear fashion and to write papers with complex sentences. This was fine for research papers, which allowed rereading of complex sentences. Unfortunately this tendency to complexity has spilled over into our preaching. Few of us have developed an "ear" for the spoken word. Our sentence structure is too complex to be listened to. We have no rhythm, and this comes across as having no soul. We just cannot write talking.

One Sunday, many years ago, I left my sermon notes in my office. It was well into the service before I realized my mistake. I had to "talk" my sermon. The sermon went amazingly well. The sermon reflected normal speech, with simpler transitions, having more in common with conversation than a research paper. The sermon was shorter since I could only say what I could remember. I discovered that those listening could only assimilate what I could remember. I even had a little style—I had soul! Packing information ever more densely on note cards was a waste of time and spirit.

How can you learn to write "talking"? First of all, vow to leave your note cards or manuscript in the office. This is particularly true if you are "hiding" behind them or if you are packing them with information in order to call attention to your eloquence. Then try to watch comedians on television. They are the great public speakers of our time. Notice how they "hook" the audience. (I would not recommend that you copy their language.) Second, find some recordings of great poets reading their poetry. Listen to them as you drive. Even if you don't understand the point of their poems, their cadence and rhythm will influence your preaching. Finally, listen to some jazz or rock and roll. The music will help you catch the beat that communicates.

41

Discover Your Church's Genetic Code

❋ ❋ ❋

Your church has a genetic code that has profoundly affected its development. You can discover this code by investigating your church's
history, interviewing older members, and taking
an objective look at how the church functions.
When you first arrive, being an outsider gives you
a perfect vantage point to view your church's
functioning.

I once served a church that had a strong German heritage. I was surprised to discover that the
entire congregation was made up of teetotalers. In
fact, some of the people could still locate the
pledge they signed as a part of the Temperance
League. I discovered that one of the founding families had left Germany trying to get a new start

because of the alcoholism of the father. The oral history of the family said that this father was greeted by drinking buddies as he disembarked from the ship after the long voyage across the Atlantic. He died young because of his alcoholism. The mother instilled strong anti-drinking sentiment in her children. The descendants of these children were now members and leaders of the church.

Obviously, this church's genetic code came out strongly against drinking, but there was more to it than that. This church had a long memory and before any new program could be initiated this history had to be consulted. Wisdom resided in the memories of the people passed down through the generations. Other churches have, of course, different genetics. One church I know about seems intent on sacrificing a minister to every building program. Yet another church seems to be unable to go more than five years without a major church-splitting controversy. Still another seems to focus discontent on the education assistant staff position, no matter who holds that position.

Understanding your church's genetics will help you understand what type of body you are dealing with. Having a mental picture of your church's genetic code will help you understand how to deal with the challenges and changes you will face.

Everyone Is an Idiot Savant

ℑmagine this scene: You're sitting in a high-powered church meeting. The committee is filled with highly educated individuals: physicians, professors, attorneys, and business leaders. These people were hand-picked by you for their intelligence, educational background, and ability to run great enterprises. You reasoned that if a person could manage a multinational corporation or perform brain surgery, he or she could operate effectively on a simple church committee. However, the meeting is not going well. Everyone is talking at the same time. No one is listening. The agenda is a forgotten slip of paper. The chair, who is a bank president, is staring off into space. How can a person who can run a bank not run a church committee meeting?

I recall meeting with a church's administrative board for their first meeting of the year. Snow and ice storms had caused the cancellation of the first three worship services of the year. Since there was no offering for three Sundays, the church's checking account was nearly empty. But the people on the Administrative Board seemed to be in the mood to spend money. I explained that there was no money in the checking account. Several otherwise intelligent people looked at the church's proposed budget and pointed out that there was money set aside for just the purpose they were advocating. Time after time I explained that just because there was a budget item didn't mean there was any money in the bank. How does this happen?

I have come to take comfort in the realization that most people are idiot savants. This means that they are brilliant in one area, but are somewhat lacking in almost every other area. Ministers may be idiot savants too. Our "savant" area lies in the ability to steer people to the best ends for the church as a whole. (For instance, you can use your ability to steer the meeting back on track, without letting the chair know you're doing it.) Although you might from time to time wish your expertise were in another field, you are a ministry savant. You can lead the church. Brain surgery you can leave to others.

43

Like Nailing Jell-O to the Wall

Some wise person has said that keeping change in place is like trying to nail Jell-O to the wall. If you've ever tried to keep all your innovations going at a church, you'll probably recognize the Jell-O metaphor as particularly accurate.

One of the core values you bring to a church is the belief that you are a catalyst for change. To this end you initiate a variety of innovations to make your congregation more faithful and effective. You may try to improve the worship service, pouring time and energy into the worship life of your church. While instituting these innovations, however, a new need will inevitably claim your attention. Perhaps it's the need for a new small group. At about this time the youth director will quit, and there will be much hand-wringing about the future of the youth ministry. Now with your focus on the need to replace a staff member, some of your worship innovations slide to become more predictable than innovative.

There are tremendous forces at work to keep the status quo. Even while you work at being a change agent, you must remember that even change changes. Remember that the very worship service you are trying to improve was once some- one else's innovation. While there are some deci- sions, such as new carpeting, that you can make once and "nail to the wall," other decisions such as worship or small-group life will require constant monitoring. You will never be "done" with them because even as you make changes, everything else is changing too. In certain living and dynamic areas of church life, you must come to peace with the idea that there will be no finish line.

The Future Is Not Just Out There, but in Your Heart

𝔉or years I thought the future was static, a target to be hit. Further, I thought those who succeeded or did well were those who had figured out where the target was and were therefore able to hit the bull's-eye. I, on the other hand, was sure that once I had loosed the arrow, someone had moved the target.

Only recently did I come to realize that the future is dynamic and is not like a stationary target at all. The future is being made every second of every day through a myriad of decisions that you and many others make. The root of the word *decision* is "to cut." How purposefully and wisely you travel *after* any decision has almost as much to do with the outcome as the initial decision itself.

Ministry Isn't a Hard Job;
It's Simply Impossible

❀   ❀   ❀

I can remember driving to church on a hot August day. At 8:30 in the morning, the thermometer already hovered in the mid-eighties. The air conditioner in my van was waging a mostly losing battle against the heat and humidity of the midwestern summer.

The climate inside the church was oppressive as well. Attendance was down; the summer vacation exodus was in full swing. Money was in short supply. Those who did attend worship seemed more prone to bicker and find fault than usual. I felt like all my efforts yielded a big fat zero. I considered looking for a new job. I longed for a job with more tangible results. I wanted to find someplace to work where the amount of effort expended was proportional to the response. At the very least, I wanted my weekends free!

As I drove along, some force larger and wiser than me brought to mind my brief stint as a worker in a steel mill (270 days spread out over three summers). Now *that* was a hard job. There was oppressive heat, stifling humidity, and a clock whose hands seemed unmoving. I was presently traveling from an air conditioned home to an air conditioned office. This was something about my present job I should have been thankful for.

Compared to working in a steel mill, ministry is not a hard job. Many of the stresses we have, we place on ourselves. We often worry how our efforts are perceived, and since we cannot control another person's perceptions, we ministers often end up angry and frustrated.

Here is a secret truth: ministry is impossible. Since the Great Commission, which challenged Jesus' followers to make disciples of the whole world, failure has been built into the system. By my count, we fail billions of times a day. Ministry is an impossible job, but the Bible counsels us that

God likes to work in impossible situations. If you accept the impossibility of ministry, you might just find the comfort of God.

"Bang! Bang! Bang!"

✳ ✳ ✳

It has been said that nothing focuses a person's thinking like knowing one is to be hanged on a certain date. Although I've never been in line for a hanging (at least as far as I know), I think I can appreciate the sentiment of the saying. At one of my charges, church life was going on as normal; in fact it was going really well. Worship attendance was steady, finances were strong, and several families were lined up to join the church. There was a feeling of harmony and hopefulness in the congregation that was particularly gratifying. That's exactly when the three shots rang out, shattering the harmony of the church.

The first indication that something had changed in the neighborhood that surrounded the church came when eight cars in our parking lot were burglarized. Then one Sunday morning two men entered the building, presumably to find something to steal. They were surprised in their travel through the building and ran away, only to rob the Lutheran church in the next block.

These activities made the church membership feel ill at ease and vulnerable. To combat this growing feeling, a security company was hired to patrol the church grounds during Sunday services and evening meetings. One night the security guard surprised three men knocking out the hinge pins of a door in a darkened section of the Christian Education building. Three shots rang out, fired at the guard by the intruders. Inside the building, a Brownie Investiture was taking place in the fellowship hall and the Christian Volleyball League was playing in the gym. It would have been just a matter of minutes before three armed men were inside the building. Fortunately no one was hit and two of the three intruders were caught by the police and put in jail. (Sadly, the two young men captured were barely old enough to drive. Sixteen is young to experience jail.)

While there was no hanging, there was a slow

choking feeling among congregation members as we experienced the reality of being cut off from our spiritual life. As a church we realized how important and how precious it was just to be able to gather. Before the shooting, gathering had been taken for granted. For the first time, we had to consider how we could maintain the integrity of our sacred space while still allowing for outreach. Could the church still be a "sanctuary" without becoming a fortress?

Our hearts did grow as a result of the night when shots were fired. We realized that being a believer was not a benign activity. We discovered that there are forces literally on our doorstep that would try to choke out the church's existence.

I have been changed in the process as well. Now when my wife asks me how my day went, I can answer with a new perspective—"At least nobody got shot." With that answer, believe me, I feel blessed.

47

You're Not Invincible. Take a Break

This is a truth that you probably didn't learn in seminary. If you were taught it, you were probably too filled with youthful enthusiasm to allow it to sink in. So now is a good time to move it to the forefront of your thinking.

Throughout history, every culture has produced ways to escape the restrictions of reality. Consider how much effort has gone into the production of wine in France and California. Recall how the youth of America were encouraged to "turn on to drugs" in the 1960s. In fact, during this period reality was defined by some as the place inhabited by people who couldn't take the drugs. It is amazing to consider how much passion, brain power, and money has gone into the perfection of heated baths, virtual-reality games, vacation getaways, mind-altering substances, and sexual adventures. Our present society is no exception, building on and perfecting what has been handed down to us by cultures in the past.

As a pastor, you must recognize this drive in yourself. But you must also realize that the escapes available to you are more limited than those available to the rest of society.

I would suggest that you actually plan your escapes. Planning some escapes will help ensure that you are not ambushed in some inappropriate way by the long-standing need to depart from reality. You are not invincible. The landscape of ministry is littered with the wrecked careers and shattered lives of people who believed that they could function without giving in to the need to escape reality. Not planning for some real and appropriate escape activities might ensure that one day you will take a long and possibly permanent break from ministry.

48

Be Kind to Your Family:
They'll Be the Only Ones
to Visit You in the Nursing Home

The most challenging part of your ministry will come when you turn into the driveway after a hard day's work. Although you may have little energy or desire for the challenge, you must try not to leave your entire heart at church.

Once, after a particularly trying day, I returned to the parsonage. The house was built so that you could enter the basement through the garage. The main hall that connected the children's rooms to the kitchen and living room ran over the garage. Often I could hear the sound of scurrying feet belonging to excited children as I entered the garage.

On this particular day, I thought I could discern even more scurrying than usual. As I opened the door I heard my oldest son say, "Should I get the fire extinguisher or not?" To be quite honest, my first impulse was to go back through the garage, get back in the car, and make a "pressing" hospital visit.

As it turned out, the fire was minor, involving some bits of leftover and forgotten casserole on the bottom of the oven. It burnt itself out without my son's having to use the fire extinguisher. Yes, it is true that God's call on your life is pervasive and all-encompassing. At some level God has probably called, or at least prepared, your family for your ministry. But part of your calling must be to act as pastor to the members of your family, and to protect them.

There will be times when your position in the church will be intoxicating. People will hang on your every word. Your efforts at spiritual growth will bear fruit. You will be overjoyed to be a part of God's plan to reclaim a lost planet. By comparison, your family's life will probably not be as thrilling. They will not experience your "highs" directly, but they will live with you through every minute of your "lows." By the time you move once or twice, your efforts in a congregation will be a distant memory. Not one person who filled the pews, enthralled at your preaching eloquence, will visit you in the nursing home.

So don't be discouraged if you have to "walk through the fire" for your family. It will be worth it. Though you may want to carry a fire extinguisher.

49

Every Once in a While, Go Deep

𝕴 received this bit of advice on living church life from an unlikely source—Terry Bradshaw's induction speech at the Pro Football Hall of Fame. For sheer joy and exuberance, his speech is hard to beat. Parts of it are often shown as part of the Hall of Fame's annual induction ceremonies. You should try to find this speech and listen to it. It will leave you with the nagging desire to have the joy and passion for ministry that Bradshaw had for football.

During his career with the Pittsburgh Steelers, Bradshaw was known for his hard-nosed play and for his ability to lead his team to victory with last-minute passing heroics. Teammate Lynn Swan was often the target of Bradshaw's passes. In the speech, Bradshaw told of being in the huddle with Swan. No matter what play was sent in by the coach, Swan always wanted to "go deep" and begged Bradshaw to throw a long pass to him. Often Bradshaw gave in and let Swan run as fast as he could so Bradshaw could throw the ball as far as he could. As a result, many times there was a dramatic outcome to their efforts.

In the ministry, most of our activities are predictable and mundane. Each week there are sermons to prepare, bulletins to be printed, and meeting agendas to be developed. Joy and fulfillment *can* be found in these seemingly ordinary activities, but every once in a while it is important to "go deep" trying for something risky and extraordinary.

I remember being at a conference and being totally enthralled by one speaker—a well-known theologian. I decided to "go deep" and invite him to speak at my church. This was a stretch—the church was no megachurch and our town didn't even have an airport to ease his travel plans. To my utter amazement, he said yes. His time at the church was a time of great spiritual growth. Many lives were changed, including mine, and I believe his life was touched as well.

Every once in a while, emulate Bradshaw and Swan and "go deep." Stretch out beyond your usual expectations. Even if you don't always score, your soul will be better for it.

50

The Body of Christ Has
an Immune System: Learn to Trust It

❀ ❀ ❀

The immune system of the human body is a powerful ally in the maintenance of good health. People with weakened immune systems are some of society's most vulnerable people. The tiniest germ or weakest infection can threaten their very lives.

Basically, the function of an immune system is to determine what belongs to the body and what doesn't. A healthy immune system, once it identifies an intruder, attacks that intruder, attempts to destroy it, and ultimately rids the body of the threat. It doesn't matter whether the invasive agent is a virus, a colony of bacteria, a splinter, or a transplanted heart.

The body of Christ has an immune system as well, and it can function just like the immune system in a human body. A wise pastor learns to trust and to use this powerful ally in the production of healthy congregations. Throughout the course of your ministry, there will be people who function like viruses, trying to make the entire church body sick. They can be a real "plague" and torment congregations for years. These chronically unhappy people can hang on for years, sapping the strength and vitality of your church.

Often it falls to the pastor to finally confront these people, but sometimes counting on the church's immune system is a wise thing to do. In other words, you needn't do it alone. I recall one church member who was a one-man plague. No matter where unhappiness broke out in the church, he was sure to be nearby. He happened to be wealthy as well and used the threat to "leave and take my money" as a way to keep the body of Christ in line with his wishes. One time at a board meeting, he used his usual threat to leave with his money. Calmly I said, "There are some things you just don't say in a group like this. Threats like that are one of them. If you don't like it here, perhaps you would be happier at some other church." The board stood firm during the meeting and even during the predictable and angry phone calls that followed from the unhappy church member. He left the church. The immune system had worked, and a period of harmony and even financial growth descended upon the church.

Watching the church's immune system work is not always pretty, but if you are patient it can nullify the toxic effects of an unhappy church member. If someone consistently works against your church's best interests, losing that member is nothing to lament.

51

The Gospel Needs No Props
or Gimmicks

❋ ❋ ❋

Anyone who has taken a pastorate knows a little bit about revitalizing a church through the pastoral energy that I call "body heat." Pastors usually "turn up the heat" when they first arrive at a church. This usually involves a round of visitation, committee reorganization, worship innovation, and effective sermonizing. Some pastors can generate enough heat to last for years. To this end, I have seen pastors preach from the church roof if certain attendance goals are met or ride a horse to church if the budget is supported at a certain level. Fortunately, this heat cools off. Then comes the real challenge: that of replacing heat with substance.

Pastors say that the gospel has the power to

change lives and even the whole world. Unfortunately, a lot of us live as if this weren't so. We tend to believe in our ability to program, market, and sell the gospel. A great deal of time and energy is spent making the message appealing and even entertaining. We act as if the gospel just won't work without our spin. At some point, we must give up on self-generated body heat in order to allow something supranatural to manifest itself.

This might be an excellent time to read and reflect on the parable of the sower from the perspective of being a preacher of the gospel. The preacher, like the farmer in the parable, doesn't always scatter seed in the most competent and effective manner. Fortunately, the harvest is not totally dependent on the sower, but rather is assured by the quality of the seed. The parable demonstrates that good seed brings forth a miraculous harvest. Good seed brings forth bounty no matter how effectively or ineffectively it is sown. It is time to trust the power of the gospel.

52

If the Pilot Lands the Plane Safely, the Passengers Will Be Safe as Well

Once I was invited to attend an evening men's meeting at a church. It was a fairly predictable affair—some food, a prayer, a business meeting, and a program. The program consisted of slides taken by a commercial airline pilot from the cockpit of his plane. He projected the slides on a large screen and showed a beautiful collection of sunrises, sunsets, and cloud formations. The pilot narrated the slide show and detailed how the beauty and design captured in the pictures had informed and strengthened his faith in God.

After his presentation, there was a brief time for questions. One man in the audience asked, "How do you live with the stress of being responsible for the lives of the passengers?" The pilot's answer was remarkable. He said, "I find that if I just concentrate on getting myself there safely, when I look behind me, all the passengers are safe as well."

I was stunned by his answer and its application to ministry, although through the years I have tried to evade the implications of his insight. Somehow the health of the pastor's soul is directly linked to the safety of his or her congregation. If the pastor is on an authentic spiritual adventure, the congregation will prosper. If you are able to deliver your soul safely, chances are when you look back, those behind you will be safe as well.

About the Author

Kurt Schuermann was born and raised in a working class family in St. Louis County, Missouri. He attended William Jewell College, where he majored in English and received the call to enter the ministry. His response to this call was to attend Harvard Divinity School. Since his graduation and ordination into the United Methodist ministry, he has dedicated his life to churches in rural and small-town Missouri.

He writes as a hobby and has published in a variety of places. His article "Asleep for My Baptism," written for the *Circuit Rider* magazine, was included in *The Best of the Circuit Rider's First Decade* (United Methodist Publishing House, 1987). A sermon he prepared while living in Cuba, Missouri, was included in *Best Sermons*, volume 6, published by HarperSanFrancisco in 1993. Most recently he produced a Lenten study for the

United Methodist Church titled "Meet the Risen Christ."

Kurt has been married for twenty-two years to his wife, Carol, who is a teacher and the editor of all his writing. His family includes two sons, Erick and Drew, a daughter, Dana, and a large golden retriever named Lucy.